Heavenly Realm Publishing
Houston, Texas

No part of this book may be reproduced, stored in a retrieval system, or transmitted by any means, electronic, mechanical, photocopying, recording, or otherwise, without written permission from the author.

Copyright © 2013 by, LaJohna Newbould, *Poems from The Heart,* all rights reserved.

ISBN—13-9781937911-61-4

Library of Congress Control Number— 2013917048

This book is printed on acid free paper.

Printed in the United States of America

Unless otherwise indicated, all scriptures quotations in this book are from the King James Version of the Holy Bible.

Published By: Heavenly Realm Publishing
PO Box 682532
Houston, Texas 77268
Toll Free: 1-866-216-0696
Fax: 281-520-4059

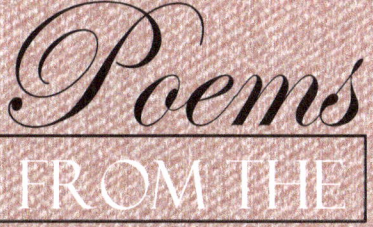

LaJohna Newbould

DEDICATION

This book of poems is dedicated first and foremost to my Heavenly Father, His Son, Jesus Christ, and the Holy Spirit. Second to my husband, Jimmy, for all the hard work he has put into helping me get this book of poems ready to send to the publisher. To our daughters, our sons-in-law, and our grandkids for I love each and every one of them dearly.

And last, but not least, Stella Parten, my friend and my soul mate in Christ. She is the one who introduced me to the actual person of the Living God, not just a name in the Bible. She watched with love as I struggled to become more than just a babe in Christ, which I imagine at times must have been quite trying. She stood firmly by my side as she loved, encouraged, and even corrected me on my journey. So with love and appreciation I give her my thanks. Thank you, Stella, from the bottom of my heart.

POEMS FROM THE HEART

As You and I come together,
My heart wells up in my soul.
It is You I want to be with.
It is You I want to know.

For when Your love encompasses me,
words spill forth from my heart.
They speak of Your love for me
and mine for You in part.

There will come a time when my heart will belong only to You,
but for now I will face each day as it comes.
Each poem from the heart I have written,
I believe came from the heart of God's only Son.

TO THE READERS

The decision to follow Jesus is the most important decision you will ever make. Although that decision will not remove you from all the problems that life brings, it does assure you of the Lord's presence in that life.

I pray that as you read these poems each and everyone will bless, inspire, and cause you to seek a deeper relationship with Him. Make the thoughts, circumstances, and feelings your own. Read them as if the Lord is speaking directly to you, because He is.

TABLE OF CONTENTS

DEDICATION
POEMS FROM THE HEART
TO THE READERS

THIS SEED   **7**
THE CHOICE   **8**
"IT IS FINISHED"   **10**
HEAVEN'S DOOR   **12**
CARRY ON   **13**
"I LOVE YOU"   **14**
WHAT IF?   **16**
GOD'S LAND   **17**
ALWAYS A TOMORROW   **18**
FRIENDS   **19**
THE CHRISTMAS STAR   **20**
LITTLE LOST LAMB   **21**
LIFE   **22**
FULL TO THE BRIM   **23**
THREE LITTLE WORDS   **24**
MY HAND IN YOURS   **25**
MY HEART'S CRY   **26**
DAUGHTER'S MINE   **27**
LIFE'S HIGHWAY   **27**
BY HIS SIDE   **30**
JESUS AND I   **32**
THIS CHILD   **33**
IT IS TIME   **34**
THIS MAN   **35**
FORGOTTEN CHILD   **36**

THE WALL   37
HE WOULD DO IT ALL AGAIN   38
GOD'S WRATH   39
MY CHILD   40
WITH THE WIND IN YOUR FACE   41
STOP AND LISTEN   42
YOUR VESSEL   43
YOU ARE NOT ALONE   45
DON'T CRY FOR ME   47
JESUS BOY   48
UNTIL THE VERY END   49
PICK ME UP, DADDY   50
IN A QUITE MOMENT   51
WHAT WOULD JESUS DO?   52
GOD'S ONLY SON   53
OUR HOPE   54
DADDY   55
THANKFUL   56
IN GOD WE TRUST   57
SILENT AND STILL   58
THE BRIDE   59
THE GROOM   60
BORN AGAIN   61
MY LORD   62
THE MAN FROM GALILEE   63
ENGRAVED IN STONE   64
I AM SECURE   66
SILENT REMINDER   67
FRESH AND NEW   68
MY DAD   69
UNCONDITIONAL LOVE   70

THE CROSS 71
NO ONE AT HOME 72
THE TEST 74
I DO 75
BLOOD BOUGHT CHRISTIAN 76
REMEMBER ME 77
"UNTIL DEATH" 78
I AM IMPORTANT TO YOU 79
HELP ME, LORD 80
YOUR GUIDE 81
PRIDE 82
FACE TO FACE 83
HIS LOVING EMBRACE 84
THE GRAVE 85
A LOVE THAT LASTS FOREVER 86
YOU WIN 87
MY HAND IN HIS 88
THE LIGHT 89
BY MY SIDE 90
JESUS IS ALIVE 91
MARRIAGE PRAYER 92
HE SAW ME 93
A LIGHT 94
IN YOUR CARE 95
HAD TO LET ME GO 96
WELCOME HOME 97
IN MEMORY OF JACK NEWBOULD 98
HIS TABLE 99
SOLACE 100
IT IS TIME 101
MY GIFT OF LOVE 102

THE HEART **103**
DEATH **104**
I CHERISH **105**
HOLD ME **106**
THOSE MEMORIES **107**

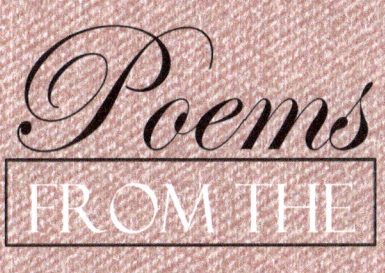

THIS SEED

You died on the cross so I might live,
so unto You my life I give.
Guide me, teach me, show me the way,
I want to please You day after day.

Joy, hope and peace of mind,
belong to me and all mankind.
I put my trust in the Lord above,
He showers on me the most perfect love.

He takes care of my every need,
so unto Him I will plant my seed.
This seed will help the world to know,
that to reap you first must sow.

THE CHOICE

When the road we are traveling, suddenly comes to an end,
there is no time to ask Jesus, to free us from our sin.
So when we stand before the angel, that holds the "Book of Life,"
our entrance into Heaven depends on our acceptance of Jesus Christ.

The timing is not ours to choose as to whether we live or die,
the choice we are allowed to make is whether or not we believe in Jesus Christ.
The time that we leave this earth may seem so very sad,
but if we have accepted Jesus, our sad can be turned to glad.

We look at things that take place through our human eyes,
then we cry out in our sorrow "Oh! My God! Why?"
The answer will never be known by us till thru Heaven's gate we pass,
then understanding will come; it will come to us at last.

The Lord's ways are not ours to understand. We just take His hand and hold on,
and know He is working on our behalf to bring us to our Heavenly home.
When you look around and are saddened by the things you see,
remember God sent His only Son to die for you and me.

Now take that step the choice is yours and a choice has to be made.
When the "Book of Life" is opened, is your name inside engraved?
Or will the angel look inside and say, "I am sorry your name is not here."
Then the look upon your face will change; change to one of great fear.

The outcome does not have to end that way the choice is still yours,
accept Jesus as Your Savior, as your Redeeming Lord.
He will open His arms to you so very, very wide,
then clasp His hands and close the circle with you safely inside.

"IT IS FINISHED"

Jesus died for you and me,
on a cross at Calvary.
He gave up His life's blood,
on the ground where sinners stood.

He looked out at the people there,
He could see most did not care.
He looked again and saw their sin,
knew He had to stay until the end.

He hung there in all His agony,
knowing He could say, "Father, come get Me."
He chose to stay on that old cross,
so the souls of man would not be lost.

He looked and saw His mother crying,
knew she did not understand why He was dying.
He looked and saw Mary standing there,
it gave His heart a lift to know she cared.

John was there with tears streaming down his face,
Jesus knew he did not want to be at this place.
But down deep Jesus was glad he was there,
it gave Him strength to know someone else cared.

Poems from the Heart

He looked out at the people with tears in His eyes.
He knew it was time to give up His life.
"It is finished," He said, and His soul departed,
the end had come to what the Father had started.

His life was required so we might live,
eternal life, to us, by His death He did give.
He died, He arose, He showed us the way,
our footsteps are firmly planted on His path to stay.

HEAVEN'S DOOR

When our time on earth is over,
and that day shall surely come.
Remember there is Jesus,
He is the only One.

He is our answer to salvation.
He is the way to reach our God.
He will stand at Heaven's doorway,
to welcome us with open arms.

All we have to do is believe in Him.
Know that He died for us.
Know that He rose from the dead,
give Him all our trust.

There is such a simple solution,
to have the best of everything.
To know that He is our Lord and Master,
to know that He is our King.

To open up Heaven's door,
and by His blood I am welcomed in.
Thank you, Jesus, for loving me,
and for freeing me from my sin.

When that final day has come,
I will be holding my arms out to You.
Knowing with full confidence,
Your arms will be out, too.

CARRY ON

That most hurtful day has come and gone,
now your life you must carry on.
"How do I do that?" you say,
I know of no other way.

Accept the blood of Jesus Christ,
read His Word and take His advice.
He will show you what to do,
pretty soon the sun will come shining through.

It won't be tomorrow or even the next day,
but just hang on He will show you the way.
When the hurt seems more than you can bare,
remember God sent His Son to show how much he cared.

He knows your pain and your sorrow, too,
He knows exactly how to help you through.
He will show you the light at the end of the way,
He will make it a little brighter day by day.

His love for you knows no bounds,
His word is strong and it is sound.
He only wants you to come to Him,
He will give you the peace that comes from within.

Take His hand, walk through this storm,
He will give you the strength to carry on.
In His arms you will find complete rest,
just "Carry On" and do your best.

"I LOVE YOU"

> IN JOHN 3:16, THE BIBLE SAYS: "FOR GOD SO LOVED THE WORLD THAT HE GAVE HIS ONLY BEGOTTEN SON, THAT WHOSOEVER BELIEVETH IN HIM SHOULD NOT PERISH, BUT HAVE EVERLASTING LIFE."

"When I asked My Son the question, will You die for them?"
"Will You go to the cross and free them from their sin?"
"He did not even hesitate and with love filling His eyes,"
"He said, Yes, Father, I will go. I will be their sacrifice."

"I will stand in their place so they won't have to die."
"I am willing to become man and to give up My life."
"I know the great love You have for them."
"So, yes, I will go. I will free them from their sin."

"I love you," the Father wants to tell you time and time again.
"I love you," even though your lives are filled with sin.
"I love you," hear these words He says to you.
"I love you, through times good and bad, and I will always see you through."

When God says, "I love you," it is not a passing phase,
it comes from His heart; He speaks to us face to face.
He did not dessert us when we made the wrong choice,
He said, "I still love you," in a sweet and gentle voice.

He knows when we do right; He knows when we do wrong,
He sent His Holy Spirit to help us be strong.
But when we insist that things must go our way,
He reaches out and says, "I love you, My love is here to stay."

So when you think you have blown it and God doesn't really care,
hear His voice so firmly say, "I love you, I am still here."
"When are you going to realize, the extent of My love for you?"
"No matter what you have done, trust Me, I will see you through."

WHAT IF?

What if You had chosen not to come and die for me?
What if You had chosen not to give Your life on that old gnarled tree?
What if You had said, "I cannot go and die for them?"
"Father, look, their lives are so full of sin."

What if You had decided we were not worth the price?
What if You had decided "The Cross" was too big a sacrifice?
What if You had decided Your life in Heaven was just fine?
That You did not want to go and die for the souls of all mankind.

What if You did not look at us with compassion and with love?
What if You did not look at us through the eyes of our Father above?
What if You did not look at us and see what our Father sees?
The reason You were sent to that old gnarled tree.

What if You said to the Father? "Their sin is just too great."
What if You said to the Father? "For them there is no escape."
What if You said to the Father? "I do not want to go and die."
"I do not want to suffer all that will be nor give up My life."

How can I ever thank You for not feeling that way?
How can I ever thank You for those words You did not say?
How can I ever thank You for the love You have shown to me?
By going, and suffering, and dying on that old gnarled tree?

GOD'S LAND

I sit on the porch each morning,
and look out at this wonderful land.
I wonder why thousands of people,
think God in this had no hand.

I look at the beauty that surrounds me,
and tears well up in my eyes.
On my lap there sits a bible,
and I thank God for His sacrifice.

This beautiful land God gave us,
we should fight to hold on to.
Cherish its moral and Christian values,
and the flag that is colored red, white and blue.

When someone tries to take it away,
we should fight with all we have got.
We should put our faith and trust in the Lord,
with Him, we should cast our lot.

For He knows the truth of all things,
of this we can be sure.
So when choices have to be made,
remember God is Holy, Righteous and Pure.

He has loved us from the beginning,
He will love us in the end.
So my Heavenly Father, I thank You,
for Your Son, to us, You did send.

ALWAYS A TOMORROW

With every breath I take, I love You.
With every song I sing, I love You.
I love You when the times are good or bad,
I love You when the trials of life make me sad.

When I hear a cow lowing or a bird singing, I love You.
When I watch a squirrel eating or a deer grazing, I love You.
I love You when the thunder rolls and the lightning flashes,
I love You when the day starts in a foggy morn or ends in a fiery splash.

When I look at our kids and grandkids, I love You.
When I talk to friends and loved ones, I love You.
I love You for who You are and what You did for me,
I love You for not turning Your back on the cross at Calvary.

When I look behind and remember the things I have done, I love You.
When I look ahead and want You to be with me, I love You.
I love You when I sit on the porch and think I cannot go on,
I love You for always being there and helping me be strong.

When Your presence in my life is hard to feel, I love You.
When I am struggling and cannot seem to find my way, I love You.
I love You because You said You would never leave nor forsake me.
I love You, because I cannot do anything else. It is not within me.

Whether I live or whether I die, I love You.
Whether I am sick or whether I am healed, I love You.
I love You through all the pain and the sorrow,
I love You because in You there is always a tomorrow.

FRIENDS

Merry Christmas from across the miles,
the thought of you brings to my face a smile.
Though we have not seen each other in many a year,
remembering times past brings to my heart great cheer.

Though life and miles may keep us apart,
I still think of you with love in my heart.
We met in a faraway land,
friends we became, that was God's plan.

Our lives touched for just a little while,
God's path we did follow as we walked each mile.
I am thankful He allowed us friends to be,
a speck in time; then through all eternity.

THIS STAR

On Christmas Day a long time ago
a babe was born in Bethlehem.
The shepherds came, the angels rejoiced,
the wise men traveled from a faraway land.

They had all followed a very bright star;
one that lit up the night.
One that proclaimed our "Dear Savior's" birth.
Oh! What a wonderful sight.

They had all come to see this wonder of wonders.
This star that so brightly shone from above.
This star that marked the birthplace of the One
God had sent down with His love.

God put this star in the Heavens above,
it was a beacon to light the way.
Its brightness reached around the world,
to show us the truth, the light and the way.

As it did then, so it does now.
Its light so brightly shines.
It lights the path we are to follow.
My precious Savior my life is Thine.

LITTLE LOST LAMB

Little lost lamb, wherever you may be,
God in Heaven is searching for thee.
He is searching high. He is searching low,
into the very pit of hell He will go.

His love for you knows no bounds,
He will go wherever need be so you can be found.
He will go into the valley of the shadow of death,
He will hold your head up and give you life's breath.

Little lost lamb, look up from wherever you stand,
reach out and hold on to that helping hand.
It is coming to you from the Father above,
it is coming to you with all of His love.

This hand that is stretched from the Father to you,
has a scar in the middle where a nail pierced it through.
This hand belongs to the Son of God,
His life He returned to this earthly sod.

Little lost lamb, this man who hung on a cross,
gave up His life so you would not be lost.
Now this hand reaches down from above,
it is sent with the Father's most perfect love.

Reach out and take hold of this love sent to you,
it cost the Father everything and it cost His Son, too.
Reach out and take hold from wherever you stand,
reach out and take hold of this loving hand.

LIFE

Your life is a shambles day after day,
you keep asking the Lord to show you the way.
You sit at the table and say, "What am I going to do?"
"This problem that is facing me I just cannot get through."
"Where are you, Lord?" I hear myself say,
"please come, please help, please show me the way."

I sit and I wonder and I look around for answers that cannot seem to be found.
"Help me, Lord, this can't be right. I have no strength left for this fight."
"I know You are out there, Your word says so."
"But right this minute I feel so lost and alone."
"Won't You take my hand and hold on to me."
"I don't seem to have any strength, you see."

"I know You are there for I believe Your Word,"
"I guess sometimes life just throws us a curve."
"The problems that assail me time and time again,
make it hard for me to understand where You have been."

"You think you are doing what you are supposed to do,
and you wonder why the Lord is not helping you."
"You look out in your misery hoping to see a little light,
something to give you hope; strength for the fight."

"You are down and the count is on three,"
"God has placed all He has betting on thee."
"He knows your strength; He knows the strength of His Son,"
"He knows where two are gathered together the battle has already been won."

FULL TO THE BRIM

As I lay in bed and stare at the ceiling,
trying to figure out what I have been feeling.
My soul cries out for more of You,
I cannot sleep I don't know what to do.

Your love is the very breath my soul needs to survive.
Without You in my life, I would surely die.
The love that comes from so deep within,
wells up inside of me, full to the brim.

There is such a longing in my life,
to take Your hand and walk by Your side.
There are no words to explain the depth of my love for You,
nor to explain the peace I feel knowing You love me, too.

Oh, my Heavenly Father, I love You so,
and I want the whole world to know.
That You and I together as one,
was made possible by the death of Your Son.

THREE LITTLE WORDS

"I love You," are three little words
that seem so very small,
to express the appreciation I feel
to the One who gave His all.

These three little words sink down in my soul
and come to the top again,
filling me ever fuller
with a love from within.

Sometimes I think I can't hold on any longer,
but my arms keep reaching for You.
That is when I realize Your love is there,
filling my heart completely full.

"I love You," doesn't quite express
the depth of what I feel in my heart,
for a Savior who came to this earth
knowing He would die from the start.

These three little words
hold a world of meaning for me,
for the One who chose to come
and die at Calvary.

Though these words are so very small,
there is great depth in them.
They describe the way my Savior felt
when He freed me from my sin.

MY HAND IN YOURS

"Take my hand, Lord. Where would You like to go?
You may have to hold on tight, for sometimes I am a little slow.
With my hand in Yours, there is so much I can do,
just point me in the right direction and I will do my best for You."

"Hold my hand tight, Lord, for sometimes I stumble and fall,
but I know You are beside me and hear me when I call.
I can always count on You to give me a helping hand,
to pull me out when I get stuck in the sand."

"Lord, where are we going? The direction is not clear,
hold on to my hand and I will try to have no fear.
With Your hand in mine, there is no limit to what I can do,
I am so thankful You chose me and I chose You."

"Where are we going, Lord? What lies ahead?
Won't You tell me, so I can be prepared?
Which way, Lord? What direction do I take?
Won't You tell me, so I won't make a mistake?"

"I love knowing You are walking by my side,
knowing that no matter what I face You will be my guide.
So hold on to me, Lord, please don't let go,
take each step with me for what lies ahead I do not know."

MY HEART'S CRY

Heavenly Father, hear my heart's cry,
whatever You want of me, my best I will try.
I have my wants, my needs, my desires,
but You are the only One that knows what
my soul requires.

So when I am on my hands and knees in prayer,
remember I am only flesh and blood, and I really
do care.
As my human words reach Your ears,
look past all the pain, the sorrow, the tears.

Look past the frailty of the words I speak,
hear what my heart says and my soul doth seek.
When words fail me, as they so often do,
just hear my heart as it cries out for You.

Reach down into the very depth of my soul,
and bring forth what I need to make me whole.
Guide me down the path You have chosen for me,
for my heart already belongs to Thee.

DAUGHTER'S MINE

This morning I was looking at pictures
of when you were very young,
love welled up in my heart
as I continued with what I had begun.

Picture by picture I went back in time
and tears started coming to my eyes,
as I walked down memory lane
I remembered each of you by my side.

I miss the times when you were little
running here and there,
filled with laughter and with love
and not a single care.

But time keeps marching on
no matter what we say or do,
I just wanted to let you know
how very much I love you.

When I look at each one of you now,
I am so proud of what you have become.
Not because of earthly accomplishments,
but because of your acceptance of God's Son.

He will be with you in times of trouble
and He will always see you through.
So call on His name when you need help,
no matter what others may tell you to do?

Accept the path before you
as it is and as it was.
God knows what He is doing,
whether or not we think He does.

Mistakes were made as parents often do,
but let them become part of the past.
We cannot be right all the time
and your time is coming up fast.

So put your faith and trust in the Lord,
for those decisions you will have to make.
Use God's Holy Word as your guide
and you won't make as many mistakes.

Out of all the things in this world.
The most precious thing by far,
is your acceptance of the One
born under the Christmas Star.

LIFE'S HIGHWAY

Is there a mountain in front of you so big and so wide,
that all you want to do is to run and to hide?
Is the river that flows in front of your feet,
so filled with turbulence you just want to weep?

Do you think you have come to the end of the line?
But you still keep hoping for some kind of sign.
A sign that says the Lord has not forgotten you,
and pretty soon the sun will come shining through.

He is always there teaching us right from wrong,
He dwells in our hearts and He gives us a song.
We get stronger each day the more we let Him in,
so open up your heart, He wants to be your friend.

The Lord God of Heaven sent His Son down from above,
to convict us of our sin and to tell us of His love.
So slow down and listen to what He has to say,
and the Holy Spirit will guide you down Life's Highway.

BY HIS SIDE

Not a day goes by
that my thoughts don't turn to You,
my heart cries out in sorrow
for what You had to go through.

When I think about the agony
and the pain You suffered there,
the cross stands before me
and I realize how much You cared.

Some thought Your death would be the end,
instead it was just the beginning.
I was on the losing side,
but now I am on the side that is winning.

Some thought Your death would drive us apart,
and all would be lost.
But I have a Savior who loves me
and thinks I was worth the cost.

He looked past all of my sin
and saw deep in my heart.
He saw how much I loved Him
and that I didn't know where to start.

So He freed me from the sin
that had taken control of my life.
He did not think death, for me,
was too big a sacrifice.

Poems from the Heart

Have you ever known such a love
that put you above all else.
A love so great that He denied life;
life for Himself.

He could have called ten thousand angels
to come and rescue Him,
but He chose to stay and die
to free me from my sin.

It is hard to understand
a love as deep as that,
someone who would die on a cross
and suffer stripes upon His back.

Now He sits at the right hand of God
with love filling His eyes,
knowing the pain He suffered there
made it possible for me to be by His side.

JESUS AND I

I don't deserve Your love,
Your mercy or Your grace,
I don't deserve to stand before You
face to face.

I don't deserve to be in Your presence
free of my sin,
but with the death of Your Son,
I am now free to enter in.

I can sit by Your side and tell You
all that is bothering me.
I can sit and talk with You
tell You my hopes and my dreams.

I can count on You to teach me
the things I need to know,
as You look down and watch me
from high upon Your throne.

Jesus took my sin
so I would not have to bare the weight,
He took me from satan's grasp
with His death He sealed my fate.

He stood between me and Your Godly wrath
as payment for what I had done,
with my choice to follow Him,
You, Jesus and I became one.

THIS CHILD

Oh, child of Bethlehem, full of wonder and light,
on the night You were born a star shone so bright.
All of Heaven proclaimed this wondrous event,
for God chose this moment for His son to be sent.

The star shone so bright on that special day,
to show the shepherds where Jesus lay.
The shepherds came and marveled at what had taken place,
the wise men came and worshipped a child full of grace.

They all knew the importance of the One they had come to see,
though they did not fully understand, He came to die for you and for me.
This child God had sent would grow to be a man,
He would obey the Father and carry out His plan.

This child who was so very small,
would soon have to give the world His all.
This child that was born on Christmas Day,
would have a very important part, in our lives, to play.

This little one whom His mother held so dear,
would soon hang from a cross while she shed her tears.
This little one who nursed at His mother's breast,
would soon give life to us by His death.

From beginning to end Jesus shows us the way
that is why we celebrate His birth on this special day.
So on Christmas morning when you awake,
don't forget the One who died for your sake.

IT IS TIME

All Heaven rejoiced when Jesus was born,
even though they knew He would be ridiculed and scorned.
They knew the Father had a special plan,
and it involved the salvation of man.

This babe, who in a manger lay,
would give His life for mankind someday.
He would look out from the cross in all His pain,
knowing why the Lamb had to be slain.

His love was so great at that moment in time,
to the Father He said. "My life is Thine."
"I stand before You in all Your glory,
so You will remember the old, old story."

"You sent Me to gather Your children to You,
so they could enjoy life in Heaven with You.
Now I sit at Your right hand,
pleading for the souls of man."

"My Father, I have done what You wanted Me to,
the souls You have given Me I now give to You.
As each day passes, nearer comes the time,
when You will say, "My Son, it is time."

THIS MAN

As I look back over the years
I wonder why I could not see,
the depth of love
this Man had for me.

He did not try to hide it.
He wore it on His sleeves,
He carried it on His shoulders
for all the world to see.

He slipped and fell and could not go on.
His burden just too heavy,
but the Father had sent someone to help
His heavy load to carry.

When the end finally came,
He was all on His own,
He never once forgot His love
and now it helped Him to be strong.

His eyes took in the scene around Him.
At no time was His love greater,
than when He looked around and saw
the image of our Creator.

His eyes then looked toward Heaven.
With His love for us piercing His heart through,
and as He took His last breath,
He said, "Father, forgive them for they know
not what they do."

FORGOTTEN CHILD

My voice cries out, I am alone in my hurt,
you think you have the right to deny my birth.
I am a mistake you said, but that is not true,
the shame that surrounds me all comes from you.

You say you have the right to decide whether I live or die,
satan has deceived you into believing that lie.
He has taken the most precious, loving moment in time,
sent me to my death with that horrible line.

You proclaim from the hilltop, "Those are not my beliefs,"
but you will stand aside as they take my life from me.
"I would never do such a thing you say,"
but all the while your actions say it is okay.

You are a child of God I thought I was safe with you,
but satan has deceived you through and through.
My mom believes her rights come before mine; forgetting all the while,
God in Heaven sees all that happens to this hurting, forgotten child.

THE WALL

Lord, I feel so far away from You.
I don't know what to say. I don't know what to do.
I feel like something is blocking my path,
but I don't know what to do to get past.

Lord, I don't know what is standing between me and You.
I have tried to think, but I haven't got a clue.
I come into Your presence just like I have always done,
but something is missing. It is just not fun.

Lord, I don't want to lose what I have with You.
I don't know what to pray for, I am so confused.
Each day I feel the wall growing higher.
Help me, Lord, help me to be a fighter.

Help me hold on to the relationship I have with You.
No matter what happens or what I am going through.
Help me put problems and feelings aside
and remember it is in You I have chosen to abide.

HE WOULD DO IT ALL AGAIN

Judas came to the garden gate.
He had brought the soldiers with him.
He stepped forward and greeted Jesus.
Kissed Him as he would a friend.

As the soldiers led Jesus away,
His disciples fled in the night.
Peter denied Him three times,
before the cock had crowed twice.

Jesus was mocked, spit on, and beaten
until He was unrecognizable as a man.
Pilate wanted to let Him go,
but the people yelled, "Crucify Him."

Jesus carried His cross toward Calvary.
Along the way He stumbled and fell.
Simon helped Him His burden to carry,
but it was Jesus to the cross they nailed.

The soldiers cast lots for His clothing.
A spear pierced His side.
On that fateful day so long ago,
Jesus Christ, the Son of God, died.

As He hung on that old wooden cross,
interceding between God and man.
He looked into the sea of faces
and knew for them He would do it all again.

GOD'S WRATH

As the lightning flashes and the thunder rolls,
the sound reaches deep down in my soul.
For it was on a day such as this,
the Son of God gave His life as a gift.

He knew His Father would accept only the best,
by giving His life He had passed the test.
The souls of man now belonged to Him,
for with His life He had purchased them.

God displayed His wrath in the Heavens above
as darkness covered the land,
it was as if the sun had been covered by a great
and mighty hand.
The earth shook as the Father showed His grief,
for the one we had crucified between two thieves.

As the tempest raged in Heaven and on earth,
God in Heaven did proclaim.
This was His Son, the Lamb of God,
who was born to be slain?

The earth calmed; the Heaven's filled with light,
God had put His wrath on hold.
To give us time to accept the gift,
the scriptures had long ago foretold.

MY CHILD

I stood in front of Jesus with my head hung low,
I wanted to run and hide, but there was no place to go.
I stood before Him full of shame for the things I had done,
I wanted so to hear Him say, "My child, welcome."

I stood there trembling in wonder and awe,
I wondered as He looked at me, what He saw.
As He stared at me, my tears started to flow,
I knew this was the One I had hurt so.

I wanted to laugh; I wanted to cry,
as I realized this man, for my life, had died.
He had gone through the agony of the cross,
so my soul and yours would not be lost.

Now the time had come to face the One from above,
His very presence was filled with love.
With His nail-scarred hand, He lifted my chin,
and said, "For you, My child, I would do it all again."

WITH THE WIND IN YOUR FACE

With the wind in your face, you taught our youth
with wisdom and with love.
Never straying from the path
given you by the Father above.

With the wind in your face, you did not look back.
You steadily plowed ahead.
You kept your eyes in front of you
listening to what the Father said.

With the wind in your face He entrusted you
with our most precious gift.
We are so thankful you answered His call
for our children would so much have missed.

With the wind in your face you taught, loved and guided them
through all the problems teenagers have.
Your own desires were put on hold
to discover why someone was sad.

With the wind in your face you have given them,
a foundation as solid as a rock.
Maturing at their own pace
remembering what they have been taught.

With the wind in your face You have given to them
strength beyond their years.
Choices are now theirs to make
so put behind you all those fears.

You have done what the Lord asked of you.
He will carry you to the next place.
Now it is time to relax in His strength
with the wind in your face.

STOP AND LISTEN

Lord, help me to slow down and take a look at all You have made,
help me realize the great price that for me You paid.
Help me reach out to someone I do not know,
when something in their life has dealt them a crushing blow.

Help me reach out with tender love and care,
when the pain in their lives is too much for them to bare.
Help me gaze into their eyes and look past their frown,
to see someone hurting, but who wants to be found.

Open my eyes and my heart to discern their need,
allow me in their lives to plant a seed.
Take this person as they go on their way,
and send someone to refresh them as they go about their day.

Help me put this world's problems aside,
to stop and listen and let You be my guide.
Help me step forward with the boldness of Christ,
so I can make a difference in someone else's life.

Give me the words I need to say,
to help someone get through a very hard day.
Most important of all let me show them the light,
how salvation only comes through Jesus Christ.

YOUR VESSEL

Lord, it is such a privilege
to be a vessel used by You,
though I may not like the trial,
I am going through.

Just knowing You are beside me
every step of the way,
gives me the courage
to face another day.

When the trial is before me
I sometimes wonder why,
I figure God has left me
and I hang my head and cry.

When the trial is over
and the sun shines so bright,
I can look back and see things
that were obscured from my sight.

Once my eyes have been opened,
I stand mute in wonder and awe,
at the things God was able to accomplish
that I never saw.

Poems from the Heart

Lord, use me in a way
You have never done before,
allow me to be Your vessel
and to boldly go forth.

Give me courage, wisdom and boldness
as You send me on my way,
take my life and mold it
as You would a piece of clay.

This earthen vessel is Yours
to do with as You will,
fill it to the top, Lord,
don't let any of it spill.

YOU ARE NOT ALONE

A cross on a tree marks the spot
where a child died,
on that fateful day
his friends and family cried.

This family, Lord,
suffered not one loss but two,
they cried out in agony
for You to help them through.

Their parents collapsed inside
from the pain,
grief shoved away
the lamb that was slain.

It was too much to bare,
a daughter and a son.
What was this
the Lord had done?

When they pass the cross,
they are filled with sorrow.
They feel You took away
all of their tomorrows.

On that day
their faith jumped the track.
They are not sure
they will ever get it back.

There is a God
who can help with your pain,
and bring you
into the fold again.

Confess the hurt and anger
you have in your heart,
give the Lord a place
where He can start.

Speak frankly
and let Him know,
how the hurt
just will not let go.

How the suffering
goes so deep inside,
it is a miracle
you were able to survive.

Put it on the altar
before His throne,
take up His hand,
you are not alone.

Look at the nail scars
on His hands,
it is time for you
to trust in Him again.

DON'T CRY FOR ME

When the time comes for me to pass from life to death,
don't you cry for me.
I have gone to be with my Heavenly Father,
and the Savior who gave up His life, you see.

When life departed this body of mine,
I was safe on the other side.
My Savior held me in His arms,
as on bended knees for me you cried.

I am not dead, I have eternal life.
My Savior did that for me.
He suffered the agony of the cross,
all so you and I could be free.

Free to choose the path we will follow,
from the beginning of our lives or until death.
Our choice will fill our entire being,
permeate our every breath.

I made my choice long ago,
to follow the Savior with all my heart.
I have never been sorry for the choice I made,
for He gave me a brand new start.

I am now safe in my Savior's arms.
I am free, I can soar like a bird.
I am now where I was always meant to be,
with my Heavenly Father, Holy Spirit and the Word.

JESUS BOY

Jesus boy, Jesus boy.
They yelled at you from across the street.
Jesus boy, Jesus boy.
They taunted as if you were a freak.

These words were thrown at you,
to make you feel bad.
To make you feel all alone,
confused and deeply sad.

The words did as they were intended.
For as a boy you hurt inside.
You wanted friends with whom you could play.
They wanted to taunt and make someone cry.

Though now you may feel lost and alone,
our Savior felt that way, too.
On the way to the cross,
where He suffered and died for you.

So when things are not going right,
and satan has stolen your joy.
Count it as a blessing,
for they call you "Jesus Boy."

UNTIL THE VERY END

There is no light,
all hope is gone.
I feel abandoned,
I cannot carry on.

I have hit rock bottom,
I don't know what to do.
"Are You out there, Lord?"
"Can You see what I'm going through?"

I can't see Your face,
but I know You are there.
It is so hard to keep praying,
when You don't seem to care.

I have been set adrift,
with nothing to hold on to.
Somehow I know if I can find You,
You will get me through.

It is down to just You and me,
I can't get any lower than I am.
But Lord, I choose to follow You,
until the very end.

PICK ME UP, DADDY

A little girl lay in her bed,
listening to the sounds outside.
It is dark and she is alone,
and the fear wells up inside.

At school a young boy sits at his desk,
trying to contend with the pain.
He looks around and wonders,
why the other boys call him names.

A young married couple has had their first fight,
they said things that were mean and cruel.
These words cannot be unspoken,
now they do not know what to do.

Another couple older in years,
have worked hard for all their tomorrows.
Now one has passed on,
and the other is consumed with sorrow.

A young girl answers the phone,
she hears the voice of a friend.
Her heart is saddened and she cries,
as she learns another young life has come to an end.

Though the world is in turmoil around us,
and our problems will always be there.
We have a Father in Heaven,
who will listen to our every care.

Pick me up, Daddy, hold me real tight,
So the hurt will go away.
Pick me up, Daddy, carry me awhile,
till I have the strength to face another day.

IN A QUITE MOMENT

In a quiet moment,
my thoughts turn to You.
I think of all the love You have given me,
and all You have been through.

There is such a peace within,
it is hard to understand.
I am so glad I found You,
and You became my friend.

I really enjoy the time,
walking with You alone.
Gazing into the distance,
feeling right at home.

Calmness, peace and love,
well up inside my soul.
I am so glad You are my God,
for You have made me whole.

The more I walk with You,
the more I come to realize.
Just how much I love You,
so very deep inside.

Just being in Your presence,
is more than I could ever ask for.
Oh! How I love loving You,
now and forever more.

WHAT WOULD JESUS DO?

One day You came along,
and took me by surprise.
For I fell in love with You,
as I gazed into Your eyes.

Your compassion was so real,
Your love so great.
Your feet so firmly planted,
no matter what Your fate.

I remembered the road You walked,
on the way to the cross.
I cringed at the way You suffered,
so I would not be lost.

Now another crossroads,
and again the choice is mine.
How far do I go?
To show that I am Thine.

The decision has been made,
for me there is no other choice.
I love You too much,
to listen to another voice.

So as each day beckons,
and problems rise a new.
The question I must answer is,
"What would Jesus do?"

GOD'S ONLY SON

The Christmas tree is a symbol,
of what Jesus did for me.
When He made that long and lonely walk,
to the cross at Calvary.

The tinsel and the lights,
that cover it from top to bottom.
Shows how all of Heaven rejoiced,
at the birth of God's only begotten.

Somewhere in its branches,
hangs a nail hidden from view.
To remind me of my Savior,
and all that He went through.

It is a very special ornament,
meant just for Him and me.
To remind me of His love,
and that from sin He set me free.

It hangs there in silence,
a mute testimony of His love.
The greatest gift ever given,
by our Father from above.

The gifts that lay unopened,
under the Christmas lights.
Represent the gift of salvation,
that cost Jesus Christ His life.

So when darkness falls all around,
and you turn the Christmas tree lights on.
Just sit and gaze in wonder,
and remember God's only Son.

OUR HOPE

As I stood and gazed at the cross,
knowing what had happened there.
Tears streamed down my face,
people laughed at me and stared.

But I knew love had stumbled all the way,
falling down, then getting up.
His burden so very heavy,
knowing this was His cup.

The Father had placed it before Him,
He knew all that it entailed.
Still He chose to drink it,
so to the cross He was nailed.

I was the cup He had accepted,
I was the one He went to the cross for.
With that one act He changed my Life,
now and forever more.

Love had taken the challenge,
staying from beginning to end.
Drinking from His cup fully,
He freed me from my sin.

"It is finished," His voice cried,
as His body gave up the Ghost.
From death to life in three days,
in Him we place our hope.

DADDY

When a man passes on, he leaves a memory,
to friends and family so dear.
If he has done his job completely,
death will have no fear.

For a man is to lead his family,
to lay their lives at the foot of the cross.
For in Heaven they will all be reunited,
and all will not be lost.

He leads ever so gently,
with a firm but steady hand.
He holds his children lovingly,
but expects obedience to his commands.

His wife is a part of himself,
she is placed above all others.
She holds the second place in his heart,
for the first belongs to our Heavenly Father.

Our Heavenly Father gives him direction,
just as he does his own.
He tries to guide them down the path,
to the Father by way of the Son.

His love is unconditional,
it comes with no ties that bind.
That is why I call him "Daddy,"
the best friend a child could ever find.

THANKFUL

As the sun dips into the ocean,
its last rays lighting up the sky.
I know I have finished another day,
with You close by my side.

I can go through any trial,
with You holding my hand.
Whether or not I like it,
whether or not I understand.

Each step I take brings me closer to You,
though at times I back up for a while.
Then understanding comes from within,
I am so thankful to be Your child.

You never leave me alone,
although sometimes I think You do.
I can learn from every trial,
if I will put my faith and trust in You.

Let me put my hand in Yours,
and follow wherever You lead.
Give me the strength to take the path,
You long ago decreed.

Let me live each day You have given me,
and quit worrying about tomorrow.
For it is in You I am complete,
I love You Heavenly Father.

IN GOD WE TRUST

A flag flies over this beautiful land,
with its colors of red, white and blue.
Love abounds in our hearts as,
we say "I Pledge Allegiance To."

As we stand in honor before it,
with right hands placed over our hearts.
We proclaim our thanks to those around us,
who for America played their part.

It is placed high on a pole in honor,
for all the world to see.
To remind us of the great cost,
of freedom and liberty.

Our sons and daughters fought for,
our friends and family died.
So our flag could fly in freedom,
over a land fully tested and tried.

She started with so much against her,
but a voice for freedom kept crying out.
As a woman gives birth to a child,
so America was born with a shout.

As years bring growth to all things,
so our country learned right from wrong.
Slowly learning day by day,
how to love and yet be strong.

It is never an easy battle,
to do what is right and just.
So as this country confronts each day,
I am thankful it is "In God We Trust."

SILENT AND STILL

The angels were there when in a manger He lay,
rejoicing at His birth.
Though they wondered why He had left Heaven,
to be part of mankind on earth.

They were there guarding the Child,
as He grew to be a Man.
Never once forgetting,
He would sit at the Father's right hand.

They were there when He was baptized,
and all of Heaven rejoiced.
For the Father had claimed His Son,
in a loud but gentle voice.

They were there in the wilderness,
when He faced satan alone.
Wanting to go forth and help,
but knowing He had to do this on His own.

They were there when He knelt and prayed,
in the Garden of Gethsemane.
As He sweat drops of blood,
His anguish they could see.

They were there as Jesus was nailed to the cross,
they watched as the spear pierced His side.
Then the angels stood silent and still,
as the Son of God gave up His life.

THE BRIDE

The bride waits nervously in the outer room,
she has been preparing for this moment her whole life.
All dressed in white she listens,
as she waits to become His wife.

She hears the music in the background,
and remembers that special day.
When she decided He was the One,
and by His side she wanted to stay.

He had always been beside her,
making His presence known.
Waiting patiently for her to accept Him,
but knowing the decision was hers alone.

As she walks down the aisle toward Him,
love fills her eyes.
As she reaches His side, He takes her hand,
soon now they will be Husband and wife.

As they take their vows in front of all,
He has claimed her as His own.
She now enjoys His protection,
His and His alone.

The bride and Groom have now become one,
she will go to live with Him.
Together they will start a new life,
while the old one comes to an end.

THE GROOM

The guests whisper among themselves,
while the music fills the air.
The Groom stands at the altar,
waiting for His bride so fair.

He keeps glancing at the door.
The one she will come through.
Impatiently His eyes search for her.
If she doesn't come, what will He do?

He wants so much for her to be there,
when all is said and done.
His heart pounds deep in His chest,
for the time has finally come.

The music stops, silence fills the air,
the moment at last is here.
The Groom turns, the door opens,
the bride finally appears.

The wedding march begins,
as the bride slowly walks toward the Groom.
She is aware of no one else,
as music again fills the room.

His love shows in His eyes,
as she takes hold of His hand.
He has waited for this moment,
before time even began.

She was well worth the wait,
she is so beautiful standing there.
She was worth the price He had to pay,
and now their lives they will share.

BORN AGAIN

Lord, I have failed You so many times.
You are probably tired of me by now.
But somewhere inside of me I keep hearing,
"Don't give up, My child."

"I took the stripes upon My back.
The crown of thorns upon My head.
I carried the cross to Calvary.
My life I gave in your stead."

"Abundant and eternal life I give.
They cost you nothing at all.
Your account was paid in full,
when you answered the Father's call."

"There was never anyone so unworthy,
nor was there anyone so bad.
That My death on the cross,
could not, in full, pay the tab."

My presence is continually before you.
I sit always at the Father's right hand.
Come boldly to the throne of grace,
for that privilege you were given when you
were born again."

MY LORD

I lay my head upon the bed,
my knees are upon the floor.
It is so nice to rest in peace,
in the arms of my Lord.

The day has not been strenuous,
nor did any trial come my way.
I just took time to stop and listen,
and hear what my Father had to say.

Sometimes I get so busy,
I don't hear Him when He calls.
He never gives up on me,
He just tries again, that's all.

Each time He becomes a little more
forceful,
but with such a sweet and gentle voice.
Whether I choose to answer or ignore,
He has given me that choice.

When I finally decide to listen,
blessings continually flow.
Nothing can compare to the time I spend,
in the presence of my Lord.

THE MAN FROM GALILEE

You wipe the tears from my eyes,
You take the hurt from my heart.
You release the pressure building inside,
You show me the path where I am to start.

You give me a glimpse here and there,
of those things that are to take place.
Lord, I will follow You anywhere,
just to see a smile upon Your face.

As You place before me,
the path I am to take.
Remove the blinders from my eyes,
so I will see what all is at stake.

Help me look past my comfort,
help me to see through eyes from within.
There are so many people out there,
who don't know You have freed them from their sin.

Give me the boldness to step forward,
and to tell them of Your undying love.
Fill me with a heartfelt compassion,
that can only come from above.

I have placed my foot upon the path,
You have chosen for me.
As unknown becomes known, as closed doors open,
my life belongs to the Man from Galilee.

ENGRAVED IN STONE

"You gaze in the distance,
and you wonder what's ahead.
Life is so uncertain,
your heart fills with dread."

There is a path in front of you,
winding this way and that.
It goes beyond the horizon,
but the courage to step forth you lack.

You raise your foot to take a step,
but fear quickly sets in.
"What ifs," quickly surround you,
what you need is a friend.

Someone you can talk to,
someone who will tell you the truth.
Someone to tell you the life you have led is wrong,
and you are living proof.

You close your eyes and hang your head,
wanting ????? You don't know what.
Crying, wishing, hoping,
pleading with all you have got.

"I will be Your friend," a gentle voice says,
as your eyes open wide.
"Just take My hand and follow Me,
I will be Your guide."

Poems from the Heart

"For I will never leave nor forsake you,
nor will I leave you alone.
For thru My death on the cross,
our lives together became engraved in stone."

So pick yourself up,
put your hand in Mine.
Put your past behind you,
there are mountains for you to climb.

I AM SECURE

The sun comes up,
light covers the land.
Another day has started, Lord,
so take hold of my hand.

With my hand in Yours,
there is nothing I can't do.
So bring forth this day,
with its skies so blue.

Help me look around,
open my eyes to see.
If there is someone close by,
who needs a hug from me.

As the day marches on,
and the sun gets low.
Put someone in my path, Lord,
a little love to show.

As this day comes to an end,
show me someone who needs a
friend.
For this day began when my hand
slipped in Yours,
great is the peace within for it is in You,
I am secure.

SILENT REMINDER

It is not the cross that hangs from my neck,
but a cross from 2000 years ago.
Where a man chose a painful journey,
for the salvation of my soul.

It hangs there in silent testimony,
of what He did for me.
The pain He suffered, the blood He shed,
all so I could be free.

If someone happens to see it,
it declares me to be the Christian that I am.
Lord, help me to live my life accordingly,
the best way that I can.

If it hangs where it cannot be seen,
I still know it is there.
It is a silent reminder,
to let me know how much He cared.

It is not an idol to worship,
nor do I pray to it on my knees.
It is just a silent reminder,
of the love Jesus has for me.

FRESH AND NEW

Lord, let me seize any unforeseen moment,
when my schedule has gone awry.
Just to talk and let you know,
I am still here and alive.

Though in my heart I already know You know,
I just want to make sure and say hi.
To let You know You are too important to me,
to give up without a fight.

So as I struggle along the way,
be patient with me when I fall.
For within each struggle I find,
I want to give You my all.

So when I am down and don't want to get up,
remind me of my love for You.
Take my hand and give a little tug,
let's start again all fresh and new.

MY DAD

Lord God above, I thank You,
for the dad You gave to me.
Steady as a rock,
sturdy as a tree.

He was always there,
when I was a growing child.
He stood beside me each step I took,
as we traveled each and every mile.

He never turned away from me,
nor did he leave me alone.
He was always there,
the backbone of our home.

Though his love was always present,
he physically was not.
His dedication to his family,
will not soon be forgot.

Lord, he did his best,
just as we all must do.
I am so thankful for "my dad,"
once again Lord, I thank You.

UNCONDITIONAL LOVE

Lord, I want to spend some time with You today,
help me to overcome the obstacles that get in my way.
Help me to spend this day with You,
so when choices confront me, I will remember Your truth.

Give me the patience to wait for Your lead,
for You are the only One who knows what I need.
Help me to take one day at a time,
to wait upon You and to let Your light shine.

As each new day dawns, help me to go forth in Your name,
to be strong, brave and bold and to not be ashamed.
Help me to feel Your presence so deep inside,
that there is no question as to who is my guide.

For You are the truth that I hold so dear,
make the path I am to follow straight and clear.
Always preparing the road set before me,
by taking my blinders off and letting my eyes see.

That as my day starts and ends with You,
Your presence will be known by the things I say and do.
Help me hold on the promise from above,
help me show others Your unconditional love.

THE CROSS

I saw You as in front of Pilate You stood,
as he washed his hands from Your fate.
As he sent You back to stand before those,
who were so filled with hate.

Each step You took brought You closer to the cross,
blood flowing all the way.
How really special I must be,
for You to have given Your life that day.

I watched as sweat was wiped from Your brow,
as tears flowed from Your mother's eyes.
As Simon took Your load to carry,
as You continued to stumble by his side.

Each time You fell my eyes filled with tears,
the agony You suffered was brought home.
I wanted to reach out and touch Your face,
but that moment was Yours and Yours alone.

As I walked up to the cross,
and I saw You hanging there.
I was so very thankful,
that for me so much You cared.

I longed to reach out and caress Your feet,
to cling to the bottom of that old cross.
To tell You how much I loved You,
and I am so sorry for how much I cost.

My heart will never forget,
all the pain You suffered there.
All so that when my body is no more,
Your kingdom I will share.

NO ONE AT HOME

I stood outside and I knocked.
No one came to let Me in.
Though I knew someone was at home.
There was no movement from within.

I just wanted to introduce Myself,
to let them know someone cared.
To let them know I was available,
their sorrows and burdens to share.

I raised My hand and knocked once again,
but no one came to the door.
I knew someone was there,
for I could see shadows on the floor.

All I wanted was to extend a hand,
to let them know a friend was outside.
Someone to show them around,
someone to be their guide.

I could hear their hearts beating,
their voices speaking low.
I wanted to tell them to hurry,
for pretty soon I would have to go.

They chose not to receive Me,
they chose not to let Me in.
They chose not to open the door,
they chose not to be My friend.

Poems from the Heart

Time has a way of passing,
their door stayed shut to Me.
When all I wanted was to be their friend,
to make them truly free.

Now it is time for Me to go,
there will be no more knocks on the door.
No more waiting for them to answer,
my call will come no more.

I have gone to be with My Father,
I have gone to be with My own.
Now if you knock I will not hear you,
for now there is "No One at Home."

THE TEST

I have sat and wondered many times,
why bad things have to happen.
Why our lives take wrong turns?
Why we go in the wrong direction?

As I think about these things,
the Lord speaks to my soul.
He lets me know it is not for Him,
it is so that I will know.

Each trial I face is a test,
just between my Lord and me.
There is no pass or fail,
it is His way of setting me free.

I will never know the answer,
if He does not put me to the test.
Whether I will stand on solid rock,
or over my body the ocean will crest.

One thing I know for sure,
His love for me is true.
And whether I laugh or whether I cry,
Lord, I will always belong to You.

I DO

The moment I said "I do",
my eyes sought Your face.
I knew there was nowhere I would rather be,
than covered by Your saving grace.

My hand sought Yours for reassurance,
as everyone looked on.
I knew I had made the right decision,
for You and I to become one.

The sun, the moon and the stars,
their brightness cannot compare to You.
You are the One I have chosen,
to spend my whole life thru.

Having You on my side,
has given me a boldness I have never known.
Being filled with Your love,
gives me comfort and strength when I am alone.

There is a confidence that fills me,
just knowing You are by my side.
I have the freedom to be me,
and it is all because You chose to die.

With that freedom comes responsibility,
a responsibility to one and all.
To let everyone around me know,
Jesus Christ is "Lord of All."

BLOOD BOUGHT CHRISTIAN

I am a blood bought Christian,
for my sake Jesus died.
He went to the cross at Calvary,
where He was crucified.

He suffered the nails through His hands,
screamed in agony as they pierced His feet.
All so when this life is over,
in His presence I would be.

He was the Son of God,
yet also the Son of man.
All that He would suffer,
was part of the Father's plan.

For the Father loved us so much,
He sent His only Son.
He opened the gates of Heaven,
by His blood our souls were won.

I am a blood bought Christian,
I will so proudly proclaim.
Jesus saved me from my sin,
by the power of His name.

REMEMBER ME

There were two crosses beside You that day,
on a hill in a land far away.
The crimes committed were crimes of a worldly life,
each filled with sin and earthly strife.

Yours was there innocent blood to shed,
for a people whose souls were dead.
The thieves cried out to You each in their own way,
did they know who they talked to that day?

"Help!" one cried out in his pain,
but for his crime he felt no shame.
He only wanted to be free from the cross,
he did not care if his soul was lost.

The other cried out "I know what I have done,
I also know You are God's Son.
I only ask that You remember me,
when entering into Thy Kingdom You will be."

Two men and the Savior were on the hill that day,
one chose his life into Jesus' hands to lay.
The thief showed men the way to be free,
by simply saying, "Lord, remember me."

"UNTIL DEATH"

What does it mean "Until death?"
I have always been afraid to be put to the test.
Would my fear over power me,
or would I stand firm and just believe.

Trust and faith seem like an easy choice,
but what happens when it is time to voice.
"Whether I live or whether I die,
I choose to believe in Jesus Christ."

Death can come in many ways,
at any time, on any day.
Will I be ready when I hear the call?
Will I stand fast and give my all?

When all I feel is fear inside,
give me Your strength and stay by my side.
Lord God, when it is time for my test to come,
help me stand fast in the name of Your Son.

Help me to put my faith and trust in You,
for others may tell me lies and untruths.
Help me to hold on to Your hand,
and to put my life under Your command.

I AM IMPORTANT TO YOU

A child has awakened before the morning light dawns,
darkness surrounds everyone and everything.
She lays there as the silence envelopes her,
knowing something has made her heart sing.

The sleepiness has left her eyes,
her heart begins to pound at a thought.
A thought that has made her soul leap for joy,
one that began deep in her heart.

"I am important to You," the thought says,
as it repeats over and over in her head.
"I am important to You, I am important to You,"
it repeats as she lies still and alone in her bed.

Her heart swells and her eyes mist,
as she realizes the Lord is talking to her.
She just wants to savor this moment,
a moment so sweet and so pure.

A time to bask in His presence,
a time to be filled with His love.
A time to just let Him hold her,
to partake in the peace from above.

"I am important to You," her heart sings,
as the Lord God of Heaven and earth lets her know.
Just how special she is to Him,
as His love for her continues to flow.

HELP ME, LORD

Help me Lord, to be faithful to You,
in all things that come my way.
Help me stay on the path that is true,
the one that proclaims "The truth,
the light, and the way.

Help me to put my best foot forward,
to let within me Your light shine.
So when people look upon me,
they know Your life and mine are entwined.

Never to be separated,
never to be lost.
You and I belong together,
no matter what the cost.

Your life You gave for me,
if necessary, now mine for Thine.
For Lord, I will trust You always,
until the end of time

Help me, Lord, be faithful to You,
in every decision I make.
For You chose to give up Your life,
and it was all for my sake.

YOUR GUIDE

Is it easy to follow Jesus?
Sometimes yes and sometimes no.
He isn't very hard to follow,
when your life is all aglow.

But when it takes a different turn,
and everything goes wrong.
When the days are cold and empty,
and the nights are centuries long.

At these times do you remember,
Jesus is wonderful, kind and good?
Do you remember to tell Him you love Him?
The way you know you should.

Or do you pull away and ask Him,
why? Oh! Why?
Or do you slip your hand in His,
and just bow your head and cry?

Gaining strength in His presence,
but weeping in His arms.
Letting His love console you,
while keeping you safe from harm.

Knowing that He is with you,
no matter the length of your trial.
Knowing He will keep your hand safe in His,
as you travel each troubled mile.

What a comfort it is to know,
He will never leave your side.
No matter what your problem,
Jesus will always be your guide.

PRIDE

Lord, forgive me for pride,
when it raises its ugly head.
Let me remember,
I belong to You instead.

Do not let it take possession,
of the way I feel inside.
Let me remember I am Yours,
and to put earthly things aside.

Let me continue to grow and learn,
that all things are possible thru You.
Lord, I want to be what You want me to be,
and to do what You want me to do.

For my will I want to be Your will,
for You know what is best.
You know what lies ahead of me,
how I will be put to the test.

You prepare me for what lies ahead,
if I will but listen to Your voice.
Always gently urging me on,
but ultimately giving me the choice.

Pride goeth before a fall,
and I don't want to fall away from You.
Lord, continue to teach me,
for my faith and my trust is in You.

FACE TO FACE

I heard Your knock many times,
but I would not answer the door.
I had many reasons why,
but I knew sin was at the core.

I did not want You to see me,
the way I saw myself.
For when I looked in the mirror,
I knew I needed help.

Sometimes in the darkness,
I would cry out in despair.
Not knowing how much You loved me,
not knowing how much You cared.

But then one day two plus two became four,
when You knocked, I said come in.
From that darkness You saved me,
and You made me whole again.

Now my life has changed,
this world is a brand new place.
It is all because I answered Your knock,
and I met You face to face.

HIS LOVING EMBRACE

A moment in time was before me,
I was unaware it had arrived.
My hand slipped from my Savior's,
and a spear pierced His side.

The look in His eyes blindsided my heart,
for a moment I could not breathe.
I wanted to take back the decision I had made,
I wanted this moment to freeze.

I wanted the past to disappear,
I wanted to erase His pain.
I wanted Him to give me another chance,
I wanted to start all over again.

And in that moment this Savior of mine,
He did just that for me.
He took all the sins I had ever committed,
and He hung them on a tree

Out in the open, in front of His Father,
His blood covering them all.
So not even one was left,
on which I could stumble and fall.

He surrounded me with His forgiveness,
He flooded my soul with His mercy and grace.
I knew once again I was forgiven,
and restored to His loving embrace.

THE GRAVE

"Jesus," the grave whispered softly,
as Judas left to do his deed.
He wanted to do things his way,
God's voice he did not heed.

"Jesus," the grave called out,
this time with a little more strength.
Jesus heard the soldiers at the gate,
His life now shortened in length.

"Jesus!" the grave called out loudly,
with glee filling his voice.
Jesus felt the nails pierce His flesh,
but because of us He had no choice.

"Jesus," the grave called out again,
his joy barely contained.
Jesus hung His head in death,
the Lamb of God had been slain.

"Jesus?" the grave questioned,
fear making his voice weak.
Jesus rose from the grave,
alive and well for all who seek.

"Grave!" Jesus answered,
in a voice mighty and strong.
"With my death and resurrection,
those who believe, to Me belong."

A LOVE THAT LASTS FOREVER

We muddle through each day,
with all its earthly woes.
Fighting the good fight,
against our spiritual foes.

We study God's word,
to make ourselves strong.
To strengthen our armor,
to discern right from wrong.

We stand our ground firm,
in our belief in the Lord.
Though those around us,
may laugh, ridicule and scorn.

We know very well,
the One in whom we trust.
Though satan may try to hide Him,
in a cloud of dust.

We choose of our own free will,
satan's bond to sever.
And to follow the One who chose to give,
"a love that lasts forever."

YOU WIN

In the darkness of the night,
fear comes slipping in.
It grabs hold of your mind,
and it settles in to win.

But in that same darkness,
a smile comes across your face.
For peace has surrounded you,
in a loving embrace.

Your thoughts go back in time,
to a man who followed a plan.
One who fought for you,
even as the nails were piercing His hands.

As you relax into His arms,
your fear you give to Him.
Knowing He will take care of you,
and no matter what, you win.

MY HAND IN HIS

I put my hand in the hand of My Lord,
going where I did not know.
Just knowing I wanted to be by His side,
no matter the path He chose.

I held His hand as we came to a valley,
which seemed so deep and so wide,
but with my hand tucked firmly in His,
we simply walked to the other side.

We next came upon a river,
raging at a fearful pace.
But peace lovingly washed over me,
as I gazed at His loving face.

My hand still in His we started to climb,
not stopping to drink or to rest.
Just pushing steadily onward,
my endurance put to the test.

On reaching the top, my Savior stopped,
and He looked straight into my eyes.
With His arms outstretched in love,
He said, "My child, you have arrived."

THE LIGHT

A voice called out in the night,
a small light pierced the dark.
Hope broke forth in an instant,
reaching out to encompass my heart.

I reached out to grab it,
to pull it close to my side.
But it alluded my grasp,
and I fell on my knees and I cried.

I could see the light in the distance,
I wondered what I could do.
To bring that light close enough,
for me to hold on to.

I kept my eyes on the light,
looking neither to the right or left.
Knowing that if I did,
my soul would feel bereft.

I stared straight at the light,
it grew brighter the closer it got.
I gazed at the One who carried it,
then I slipped my hand into the hand of God.

BY MY SIDE

In my darkest moment,
when my world comes crashing down.
When my heart grows heavy,
and my face wears a frown.

When I look around me,
and realize I am losing hope.
I see the storm clouds gathering,
and I am not sure I can cope.

The rain blows in my face,
and the wind pushes at my back.
It comes from every direction,
it gives me no slack.

Then somewhere in the darkness,
a little light I see.
It illuminates a nail scarred hand,
holding on to me.

The strength I see in that grasp,
makes me feel safe inside.
Then I know come what may,
Jesus will always be by my side.

JESUS IS ALIVE

The lion sits quietly,
watching those moving about below.
He licks his lips in anticipation,
waiting for someone he does not yet know.

He lies quietly observing,
all the things that are taking place.
Waiting for the moment,
when a wrong choice will give him space.

A moment, just a moment,
has taken someone by surprise.
The lion jumps to his feet,
showing his laziness was just a guise.

In that moment he lunges,
his aim is to devour all in his path.
He cares not about all the pain he will cause,
and at the suffering he will laugh.

As he gets closer to his prey,
he is stunned by what he sees.
For the prey he has chosen,
has fallen to his knees.

In defeat he roars loudly,
lunging wildly from side to side.
But disappearing into the darkness,
knowing Jesus is alive.

MARRIAGE PRAYER

Almighty God, we come before You,
two people choosing to become one.
We ask Your blessing on our union,
in the name of Jesus Christ, Your Son.

You know the trials we will face,
so go before us and prepare the way.
Help us put You first,
as we arise and begin each day.

For though our path will not always be straight,
we put our faith and trust in You.
All we ask is that You hold us close,
in Your wisdom and in Your truth.

As we take this step hand in hand,
and together we start a new life.
Put Your arms around us, Lord,
as we become husband and wife.

HE SAW ME

Jesus sought His Father,
as He knelt in prayer that night.
Seeking His direction,
for His body's earthly plight.

His path was laid before Him,
He saw it bright and clear.
What He saw made Him tremble,
and His body sweat blood, and cried tears.

He stood silent in front of Pilate,
as the accusations were read.
Never uttering a word in His defense,
just standing with lowered head.

His burden was so heavy,
too heavy for one man to bare.
But carry it He did,
with no one His pain to share.

The nails pierced His hands and feet,
a spear pierced His side.
In agony again He sought comfort,
from His Father's eyes.

What made Jesus stay that day,
deliver His life upon that tree.
It was when He opened His eyes,
and standing in front of Him "He saw me."

A LIGHT

I stared into the darkness,
its blackness dark and deep.
I knew not what would confront me,
but it was Jesus I wanted to seek.

Cautiously I took the first step,
my eyes darting here and there.
I wanted to know more than I did,
I wanted assurance that He cared.

I took a few more steps,
wanting my path clear to see.
But God does not always work that way,
so that was not to be.

I stepped forward once again,
waiting for Him to show me the way.
In that darkness He placed a light,
that drew me to Him that day.

IN YOUR CARE

When the sun peeps over the horizon,
and the light chases away the dark.
I gaze in wonder and awe,
as love consumes my heart.

For as I look around me,
I see Your touch in everything.
And I know that by my side,
You will always be.

The beauty that surrounds me,
speaks loudly of Your name.
As I look upon it,
I know I will never be the same.

If by chance the beauty goes,
I know You will still be there.
I will always love You,
and have faith in Your care.

HAD TO LET ME GO

Here I stand at Heaven's gate,
not understanding why.
What had happened on that earthly shore,
that had caused me to die.

I looked around bewildered,
not knowing why I was here.
I had not asked Jesus into my heart,
and now my heart trembles with fear.

I looked and saw an angel,
the one that holds the "Book of Life."
The book was now open in front of him,
and I just stood there and cried.

Many times I had been at the crossroads,
when asked to choose, I just said no.
Now the darkness has overtaken me,
to Heaven I will not go.

My soul cries out in agony,
for now I knew the truth.
But death has already claimed me,
and now there is no more time to choose.

For in choosing not to choose, I had chosen,
what lies ahead I do not know.
Then Jesus, with His heart breaking,
finally had to let me go.

WELCOME HOME

Heaven's gate is now before me,
I am filled with such inexplicable joy.
For whatever happened on earth,
I am no longer satan's ploy.

Why had God chosen this time,
to separate me from loved ones so dear.
It is a mystery unsolved by me,
but okay, because now I am here.

For I am in the arms of my Savior,
no more trials and tribulations to face.
The angel in front of me holds the "Book of Life,"
in Heaven giving me place.

When the crossroads loomed in front of me,
I stood and in a loud voice cried.
"You are my Savior and I love You,
and I know why You had to die."

In that moment when the choice was mine,
I gladly claimed Jesus as my own.
Then with His heart bursting with joy,
He said "My child, Welcome Home."

IN MEMORY OF
JACK NEWBOULD

My brother-in-law, Jack Newbould, passed away October 6, 2012 from lung cancer. The following poems were written in the days prior to and following his death.

HIS TABLE

The light is slowly disappearing,
very soon it will shine no more.
Though it is disappearing from this earth,
it will reappear on that far distant shore.

When it is time,
Jesus will take hold of your hand.
Until that time you never give up,
but when He calls, it is time to go,
it is at His table you will sup.

Nourishment will now fill your body,
from the Bread of Life you will receive Living Water.
How very lucky you are,
for you have gone to be with the Father.

Those left behind will cry,
their hearts will hurt every day.
But they will find comfort in knowing,
you are in the arms of the One who is the Truth,
the Light and the Way.

SOLACE

How to pray? I do not know,
Lord, my eyes do not see what You see.
I know miracles do happen,
so I come to You on bended knee.

Words race through my mind, but my lips remain silent,
I am so tired it is hard to think.
In my desperation I cry out,
and in loneliness I begin to sink.

The darkness of the night surrounds me,
and I wonder why things have to be this way.
The hurt I feel goes so deep,
it is hard for me to pray.

I take the Hand that is offered,
knowing it provides the solace I need.
Though I do not know what lies ahead,
it is into Your hands my cares I leave.

IT IS TIME

The time has come for a loved one to go home.
It is time for him to take his last breath.
It is time for him to go be with our Lord,
for eternal life follows an earthly death.

And though we cry and hurt inside,
there is nothing we can do.
For when it is time to meet Jesus,
we must bid this earthly life adieu.

As we look at the days in front of us,
as fear of what lies ahead consumes our minds,
we must remember we have a God who loves us,
and He is ever so patient, so loving and so kind.

So when fear tries to overcome us,
and the road ahead looks so terribly long.
Tell satan he has to leave us alone,
for it is to Jesus we belong.

MY GIFT OF LOVE

I heard your voice as you cried out,
you spoke just in time.
For it was in your acceptance of Me,
that you became eternally Mine.

You accepted My gift of love,
when it was offered to you.
Now you are free to walk with me,
as Heaven's portal you pass through.

I took your hand when you called My name,
it was time for you to leave this world behind.
Now you and I will walk together,
through the many eons of time.

THE HEART

What about the heart? What is it to do?
When the loss of a loved one now fills it with pain.
Though others may offer their condolences,
you know your life will never be the same.

You think of all the tomorrows that are gone,
your eyes cry, but tears no longer fall.
The heart keeps right on beating,
as friends and family continue to call.

You walk and talk and sometimes laugh,
but when they leave, you once again feel bereft.
You have just lost the other half of yourself,
and you begin to think there is nothing left.

You may think your life is over,
but God is holding you in the palm of His hand.
He knows and sees what you are going through,
your pain He understands.

Let Him help you through this time of sorrow,
let Him prepare the direction you are to go.
When you allow Him to work on your behalf,
He will open up a world of treasures untold.

DEATH

Death is becoming more of a reality every day,
as family and friends pass away.
The older we get and time passes on,
memories are forgotten; those that were known.

Though death is a product of man's sin,
with Jesus' death we are forgiven and are free to enter in.
For with His death He gave us the key,
for Heaven's portal we must now leave.

Though death may bring so many tears,
accepting Jesus alleviates all fear.
He is the truth, the light, and the way,
the choice is ours; the words we must say.

Life, Jesus gave when He went to the cross,
all so our souls would not be lost.
As this earthly life approaches its death,
call out to Jesus with your last breath.

I CHERISH

Lord, I give myself to Thee,
everything I am or ever hope to be.
You are the God of my choice,
I have proclaimed in a loud voice.

I love Thee with a heart that is true,
I now and forever belong to You.
I am so glad You came into my life,
I cherish the day when I became Your wife.

For now I will stay on this earthly shore,
until You call opening Heaven's door.
When that time comes, I know I must go,
but it is okay for I love You so.

HOLD ME

I awake in the night,
the stillness surrounds me.
I reach out to touch the pillow by my head,
it is empty,
my heart breaks,
so I hold it to my body instead.

My love is gone,
he will lay beside me no more.
The tears begin to flow like rain,
I am alone,
my feet touch the floor,
but I cannot get away from the pain.

It is then I cry out,
my heart hurts so.
Only You can help me through my sorrow,
hold me close,
Lord God above,
so I can believe there will be a tomorrow.

THOSE MEMORIES

A loved one has crossed over the river,
hearts have been broken in two.
Those left behind will have only memories,
they can hold on to.

Make those memories now,
for you know not when your time will come.
Spend time together with family and friends,
fill your life with the Lord, with laughter, and with fun.

As each day passes, we get closer to our leaving,
the older we get the more memories we leave behind.
Make sure those memories are filled with lots of love,
for when we go there will be no more time.

About the Author

La Johna Newbould

is a late-in-life Christian. It was not until she was in her early forties that she accepted Jesus as her Lord and Savior. She published her first book, which was a mystery novel called, "She's Mine", in 2012. The Lord has given her several poems over the years so she has decided to put them in a book called, "Poems From the Heart." She gives God all the credit and thanks Him for inspiring her to write and publish both books.

www.ingramcontent.com/pod-product-compliance
Lightning Source LLC
Chambersburg PA
CBHW070647050426
42451CB00008B/303